BIOGRAPHY OF RICHARD DEAN MCINTYRE

TABLE OF CONTENTS

INTRODUCTION

A key player in the political and judicial scene of Indiana, Richard Dean McIntyre exemplified the intricacies of ambition, service, and personal struggle. He was a prominent presence in each of these areas. He was born on October 5, 1956, and he chased his aspirations with a lot of enthusiasm. At first, he wanted to become a pilot for the Navy. His knee injuries, on the other hand, changed the trajectory of his life and led him to pursue a career in law and public service. The path that McIntyre travelled was characterised by a number of noteworthy accomplishments, such as his time spent serving as a state lawmaker and, later, as a recognised appellate court judge.

When McIntyre ran against the incumbent Democrat Frank McCloskey in a controversial election for the United States House of Representatives in 1984, he earned national prominence thanks to his performance. A close margin of victory, charges of election fraud, and a drawn-out recount process that enthralled political observers were all aspects of the contest that contributed to the high level of drama that this race featured. McIntyre's resiliency shone through in spite of the difficulties, which is a reflection of his passion to public service and his commitment to the people of Indiana constituency.

On the other hand, the story of McIntyre's life is not only defined by the achievements he has achieved in his professional life. A tragic outcome was ultimately brought about by the combination of personal hardships and the expectations that come with living a political life. McIntyre did not appear to have taken his own life when he passed away at his home in Bedford, Indiana, in October of 2007. He was 51 years old. An investigation by the federal government was being conducted into him at the time of his passing, and it was connected to a controversy that involved the improper use of military contracts. This revelation added a new layer of complexity to his already convoluted legacy.

The life of Richard Dean

McIntyre is examined in depth in this biography, which dives into the significant events that impacted his journey from a young man with aspirations of flight to a devoted public servant who navigates the hurdles of politics and law. We investigate topics such as aspiration, resiliency, and the contrasting aspects of the human experience through the lens of his narrative. The life of McIntyre serves as a powerful reminder of the influence that external demands can have on an individual's well-being, as well as the delicate balance that must be maintained between service to the public and personal integrity.

CHAPTER 1

Early Years and Goals For the Future

On October 5, 1956, Richard Dean McIntyre was born in the tranquil community of Bedford, Indiana, in the state of Indiana. His upbringing in a neighbourhood that was very close-knit instilled in him the importance of working hard, being determined, and being of service to others. The significance of education and civic duty was instilled in him by his parents, who were profoundly anchored in the traditional Midwestern ethos through their parenting. McIntyre shown a sharp intellect and a strong will to succeed from a young age, both of which would eventually define his professional path in the years to come.

Young McIntyre had a strong interest in the field of aviation from an early age. The tales of bravery and excitement that he heard throughout his childhood motivated him to have a desire of flying through the air as a pilot for the United States Navy. Not only did this aim demonstrate his desire to serve his country, but it also exhibited his sense of adventure. After completing his high school education, he went on to enlist in the Naval air training program in Pensacola, Florida, in order to pursue this desire. The knee injury he sustained while training, however, put an end to his dreams of a future in the military. This failure turned out to be a defining point in McIntyre's life, as it compelled him to reevaluate his objectives and move his aspirations in a different direction.

In the aftermath of the injury, McIntyre went back to Indiana with a newfound concentration on his academic pursuits. He attended Indiana University Bloomington, where he worked towards earning a Bachelor of Arts degree in Journalism as well as a Bachelor of Science degree in Political Science. During his stay at the university, he underwent a profound transformation; it sparked his interest in public affairs and enhanced his comprehension of the political landscape. In order to hone his abilities in communication and critical thinking, McIntyre became actively involved in university organisations and discussions. He was able to lay the framework for a career that would combine law, politics, and public service through the experiences he had while attending Indiana University.

In addition to his academic efforts, McIntyre also joined the Indiana National Guard, which was an experience that brought him closer to his prior aspirations of serving in the military. In the course of his duty in the National

Guard, he worked his way up through the ranks to become a military lawyer. In this capacity, he was able to combine his legal education with his dedication to the military. His dual path of schooling and military experience would eventually shape his attitude to politics and law, as he developed a great feeling of duty towards his society and country. This dual path would affect his approach to both of these fields.

Following the completion of his undergraduate degree in 1980, McIntyre took the important choice to continue his education and get a medical degree. Through his studies at the Maurer School of Law at Indiana University in Bloomington, he was able to acquire a more in-depth comprehension of the legal system as well as the complexities of government. During his time in law school, he began to picture a future in which he could have an impact on society through political engagement and legal advocacy. This was a significant development in his hopes towards the future.

McIntyre's work ethic and

dedication to public duty were demonstrated by the fact that he paid equal attention to his studies and the commitments he had to fulfil in the military. After graduating from law school in 1983, he was equipped with the information and abilities necessary to negotiate the difficulties of a legal career. Additionally, he emerged with a clear vision of his future, which was to serve as a voice for his constituents and a steward of justice.

During the time that McIntyre was getting ready

to enter the realm of politics, the experiences that he had during his formative years were extremely influential in forming his desires and principles. The principles that he learnt throughout his formative years, such as the necessity of education, the commitment to serve, and the ability to remain resilient in the face of adversity, laid the groundwork for a career that would be distinguished by both successes and hardships. McIntyre's adventure had just begun, and he was resolute in his intention to leave his stamp on the political scene of Indiana.

CHAPTER 2

The Starting Point for Politics

The beginning of Richard Dean McIntyre's dynamic career, which would be characterised by both noteworthy accomplishments and acrimonious conflicts, was marked by his entry into politics. Following the completion of his legal education in 1980, McIntyre made the decision to challenge for a seat in the Indiana House of Representatives. He was driven by the aspiration to bring about positive change and make a positive contribution to his community. His growing concern for the problems that his people are facing, particularly in areas like as education, public safety, and economic growth, was a driving force behind his decision to enter the political arena.

The campaign of McIntyre was distinguished by the implementation of local initiatives and a personal touch. In addition to attending local events and actively engaging with community leaders, he travelled throughout his district, meeting with voters in their homes and attending local activities. His friendly demeanour and genuine interest in the issues that were important to the public struck a chord with a great number of people. He promised to campaign for measures that would better the lives of working families in Indiana, and he positioned himself as a candidate who understood the issues that working families confront on a daily basis.

In 1980, he was elected to the

Indiana House of Representatives, representing a district that encompassed portions of Lawrence County. His dogged determination paid off, and he was able to achieve his goal. This victory was not only a significant personal achievement for him; it also marked the beginning of his dedication to public service responsibilities at the state level. McIntyre rapidly established himself as a committed politician after he was elected to parliament. He worked extensively on a variety of committees and advocated for legislation that addressed school reform, accessibility to healthcare, and improvements to infrastructure.

McIntyre's popularity among his constituents continued to rise when he was reelected in 1982. This popularity was boosted by his ability to interact with the community and effectively convey their concerns in the legislature. He frequently worked with people from other political parties to accomplish meaningful goals, which earned him recognition for his collaborative spirit. His increasing power inside the Indiana General Assembly laid the groundwork for his subsequent ambitious political move, which was to contest a seat in the House of Representatives of the United States of America.

When McIntyre competed for the 8th congressional district of Indiana in 1984, he encountered a difficult opponent in the form of the incumbent Democratic representative Frank McCloskey. The race was extremely competitive. The campaign was characterised by intensive political manoeuvring, which was reflective of the political climate that existed at the national level at the time. In order to highlight his track record of service and his dedication to the people of Indiana, McIntyre made use of his experience having served as a state representative. He concentrated on important matters such as the expansion of the economy, the development of new jobs, and the requirement for a robust national defence.

There was a lot of emotion around the election, and the stakes were extremely high for both candidates.

Throughout the course of the campaign, McIntyre encountered a multitude of obstacles, such as discrepancies in finance and the requirement to gather support from a varied electorate. He reached out to prospective voters by employing a variety of marketing measures, including direct mail, television debates, and community gatherings. He used a combination of classic and contemporary campaigning techniques.

In the beginning, the results of the election day were not

obvious. Early reports indicated that McCloskey was in the lead by a slim margin; but, a month later, when a mistake in the tabulation was discovered, McIntyre was proclaimed the winner by a scant 34 votes. As the process of recounting the ballots began in the midst of a politically tense environment, this news created a great amount of controversy. The unfolding drama brought to light the precarious nature of the results of elections and the rigorous scrutiny that is associated with political battles at this level.

The atmosphere in Washington became increasingly tense as the recount continued. A politically tense impasse ensued as a result of the newly elected House of Representatives being sworn in without either candidate being seated in their respective seats. The political tensions that existed during that time period were reflected in the fact that both parties were involved in a heated discussion regarding the legitimacy of the election process. McIntyre remained unwavering in his determination, steadfastly defending his innocence in the face of charges of improper behaviour and pledging to battle for his entitlement to serve in Congress.

In the end, the recount was completed, and it was discovered that McIntyre had, in fact, been defeated in the contest by a margin of 418 votes. The drama that surrounded the election shed light on the complexities of the political scene as well as the difficulties that are encountered by those who are attempting to serve within it.

For McIntyre, the experience he gained during this election would prove to be crucial as he handled future hurdles in his career, despite the fact that he experienced a setback.

It was the aftermath of the election when McIntyre experienced a turning point in his life. Despite the fact that he was unsuccessful in his bid for a seat in Congress, his determination to serve his community remained unshaken. After that, he transferred his attention back to Indiana, where he would continue to make substantial contributions in the areas of law and the judiciary. Not only did his journey through the political process indicate his dedication to public service, but it also shed light on the complex dynamics of electoral politics, so laying the groundwork for the subsequent chapter of his life.

CHAPTER 3

The Battle for Congress

The 1984 campaign for the U.S. House of Representatives was not just a race for office; it was a crucible that tested Richard Dean McIntyre's resilience and commitment to his political ideals. Having previously served as a state representative, McIntyre entered the race with significant experience but also faced the challenge of competing against an incumbent who had established a solid voter base.

The political landscape in Indiana's 8th congressional district was complex, shaped by economic factors, demographic shifts, and changing political allegiances.

As McIntyre prepared for the campaign, he understood that a strategic approach would be essential. His campaign team worked tirelessly to analyze voter demographics, identify key issues, and develop a platform that resonated with constituents. They discovered that concerns about the economy, job creation, and national security were at the forefront of voters' minds.

McIntyre's background as a lawyer and military officer allowed him to position himself as a candidate who could navigate both local and national issues effectively.

To distinguish himself from McCloskey, McIntyre focused on his own record of public service. He held town hall meetings, engaged in direct voter outreach, and participated in debates, all while emphasizing his commitment to transparency and accountability in government. His campaign slogan, "A New Voice for Indiana," captured his message of change and hope, appealing to voters who were eager for fresh perspectives in Congress. McIntyre's charisma and relatability won him supporters across party lines, further solidifying his position as a strong contender.

However, as the campaign progressed, the race took a dramatic turn. The Republican National Committee recognized McIntyre's potential and provided additional support in the form of campaign funding and resources. This backing allowed him to expand his reach through television ads and direct mail campaigns, significantly increasing his visibility in the district. McIntyre's message resonated, and he garnered endorsements from key local leaders, further strengthening his campaign.

The tension in the race heightened as election day approached. Voter turnout was crucial, and both candidates worked tirelessly to mobilize their supporters. McIntyre emphasized his commitment to listening to the concerns of his constituents, often visiting local businesses and community centers to engage in conversations about their needs. His efforts paid off as he saw a surge in grassroots support, with volunteers mobilizing to spread his message throughout the district.

On election night, the atmosphere was electric. Polls closed, and results began to trickle in, revealing a closely contested race. Initially, McCloskey held a slim lead, which fueled anxiety among McIntyre's supporters. As the night wore on, McIntyre's campaign team remained optimistic, believing that the late-night turnout from their dedicated volunteers would ultimately tip the balance in their favor.

When the first wave of results was announced, they showed McCloskey ahead by a mere 72 votes. However, as the dust settled, a shocking revelation emerged: a tabulation error had skewed the initial results. After a review, McIntyre was declared the winner by a narrow margin of 34 votes. The news sent shockwaves through the political landscape, and celebrations erupted among McIntyre's supporters. Yet, the euphoria was short-lived as the election results were immediately challenged.

As the controversy surrounding the election grew, McIntyre found himself embroiled in a legal battle that underscored the volatility of the political climate. Both parties sought to claim legitimacy, leading to a protracted recount process that captured national attention. The situation escalated as Democrats in the House of Representatives, led by McCloskey's supporters, initiated a motion to seat neither candidate until the recount was completed. The political stalemate reflected deep divisions within the House and raised questions about the integrity of the electoral process.

Throughout this tumultuous period, McIntyre maintained his composure, relying on his legal background to navigate the complexities of election law. He engaged with legal experts and strategists to bolster his case, insisting that the electoral process had to be respected and that the voters' voices should be heard. His commitment to transparency resonated with many, but the political ramifications of the recount proved challenging.

By the end of January 1985, after months of intense scrutiny and public debate, the recount concluded with McCloskey ultimately winning by 418 votes. McIntyre's defeat was a bitter pill to swallow, but the experience fortified his resolve. He emerged from the election battle with valuable insights into the political process and a deeper understanding of the challenges facing those who seek public office.

The 1984 election served as a formative moment in McIntyre's career, revealing both the triumphs and pitfalls of the political arena. Though he did not secure a seat in Congress, he remained undeterred and committed to public service. This chapter of his life highlighted the complexities of electoral politics and the importance of integrity, ultimately setting the stage for McIntyre's next chapter in his career as he shifted focus from national politics to the judiciary, where he would continue to make an impact in Indiana.

CHAPTER 4

A Judge's Legacy

Following the turbulent events that occurred during the 1984 election, Richard Dean McIntyre made a significant career change that would play a significant role in defining his legacy. He moved from the political arena to the judicial system. When McIntyre was appointed to the position of judge on the Circuit Court of Lawrence County in 1988, he embraced his new duty with the same zeal and dedication that characterised his prior political endeavours. Because of his expertise in law and his previous experience in politics, he was in a very advantageous position to traverse the complexity of the judicial system, which enabled him to have a big impact on the broader community.

Acknowledging and Accepting the Role of Judge

When McIntyre was appointed to the bench, it was not only a step for his career; it was also an opportunity for him to serve his community in a way that was significant. As a result of his prior experience as a military lawyer and as a practicing attorney, he possessed a profound comprehension of the law as well as the complexities of the legal process. When McIntyre first took office, one of his primary goals was to make sure that the courtroom was a place where justice was also available to everyone. Having the awareness that fast decisions were essential for those who were seeking justice, he put into action efforts to streamline case handling and eliminate delays.

As a result of his reputation for being fair and impartial, he garnered the respect of many people, including his colleagues, attorneys, and members of the community. McIntyre was a firm believer in the notion that every person deserved to be tried in a fair manner, and that the legal process ought to protect the dignity of all parties concerned. It was his courtroom that exemplified professionalism; he fostered an atmosphere of open communication and upheld decorum, making certain that every individual's opinion was taken into consideration.

Affecting the Administration of Justice in Indiana

During the course of his tenure, McIntyre ruled over a diverse range of cases, which included both civil and criminal proceedings. He was particularly well-known for his work in family law, where he addressed delicate matters such as child custody and marital relations. His work earned him a lot of respect. McIntyre treated these situations with compassion, as he was aware of the emotional burden that they entailed for the families involved. Many families were able to find resolutions that prioritised the well-being of children and encouraged cooperative co-parenting arrangements as a result of his ability to traverse complex emotional relationships.

The influence of McIntyre stretched beyond the confines of the courtroom. He participated in a wide range of legal organisations and activities that were aimed at enhancing the justice system, and he was an active member of the judicial community in Indiana. Additionally, he worked on initiatives that were aimed to assist individuals in navigating the legal process and campaigned for legal reforms that would improve access to justice for marginalised populations.

The Reelection Process and Participation in the Community

It is a testimonial to the confidence and respect that McIntyre had acquired from the town that he was reelected to his position without any opposition in the year 1990 from the community. Because of his reelection, he was able to continue working towards the realisation of his goal for a judicial system that is just and equitable. Recognising the significance of establishing connections between the judicial system and the general population, he increased the scope of his community engagement activities during the course of his career.

He frequently took part in community activities, where he presented educational workshops on the rights and obligations that are associated with the judicial system. Although McIntyre was of the opinion that a well-informed populace was necessary for the functioning of a robust democracy, he made a concerted effort to educate people about the rights that they were entitled to under the law. His efforts to reach out to the community included forming partnerships with local schools in order to teach kids about the legal system, thereby cultivating a feeling of civic responsibility and imparting an understanding of the law.

Finding Your Way Through Obstacles

Throughout his tenure as a judge, McIntyre had obstacles, despite the fact that he was successful. There were times when he found himself in the position of negotiating tough legal battles that were connected with larger societal issues. The legal landscape in Indiana was not immune to political influences, and he found himself in this position. In spite of the demands that came from the outside, McIntyre did not waver in his dedication to defending the concepts of justice and the rule of law under all circumstances.

Integrity and a strong dedication to his principles were hallmarks of his approach to judicial leadership, which characterised his approach. On numerous occasions, McIntyre emphasised the significance of judicial independence, emphasising that judges should be free from political influence in order to make decisions that are completely based on the law and the facts that are presented in each individual case. Despite the fact that he received both praise and condemnation for his dedication, he never wavered in his conviction that the judicial system ought to serve as a barrier against political expediency.

Making Arrangements for the Deployal

In addition to continuing to serve on the bench, McIntyre maintained his connection to his military heritage throughout his career. He was a member of the Indiana National Guard, where he had attained to the rank of Colonel, in addition to the judicial duties that he was responsible for. Although his twin duties as a judge and military officer demonstrated his commitment to public service, they also confronted him with a variety of obstacles that were not found in other contexts.

McIntyre was a member of the 76th Infantry Brigade Combat Team, and in the years leading up to his passing, he participated in preparations for his deployment to Iraq. For him, this time period was a source of both pride and fear at the same time. He was aware of the sacrifices that were required of those who served in the military and was determined to carry out his responsibilities. On the other hand, trying to fulfil his duties as a judge while simultaneously getting ready for deployment put a significant amount of pressure on him.

It is impossible to forget the impact that McIntyre's time spent serving as a judge in Lawrence County had on the town. In addition to being a powerful figure in the judicial system, he was also a compassionate leader who sincerely cared about the people he was responsible for serving. His career on the bench was distinguished by his commitment to justice, transparency, and community engagement; as a result, he left behind a legacy of honesty and public service.

McIntyre was confronted with apprehension regarding the future as he was getting ready for deployment. Despite this, he continued to pursue his twin obligations with the same unflinching determination that had characterised his career up to this point. The difficulties he encountered in his work as a judge would pave the way for the turbulent final chapter of his life, which would be marked by the culmination of the pressures he endured in both his judicial and military responsibilities, which would ultimately result in a tragic and untimely death.

CHAPTER 5

The Latter Years and the Legacy

Richard Dean McIntyre's latter years were marked by dramatic changes, personal problems, and an untimely tragedy that would throw a long shadow over his legacy. These events occurred during the years when he was reaching the end of his life. It was difficult for him to handle the complexity of being a judge, a military officer getting ready for deployment, and a family man all at the same time. The strains started to take their toll on him. This chapter dives into his final years, examining the events that led up to his passing, the effects of his passing, and the legacy that he left behind that will endure for generations to come.

Making Arrangements for the Deployal

The multiple duties that McIntyre was responsible for got increasingly difficult in the years running up to 2007. Not only did he feel a profound sense of obligation to serve his nation, but his dedication to the Indiana

National Guard was also a source of pride for him. It was his responsibility as a Colonel and judge advocate to provide guidance to military people regarding legal matters. This was a role that required him to strike a careful balance between military discipline and legal competence.

The fact that McIntyre had to go through training and briefings in order to get ready for his deployment to Iraq added still another layer of stress to his already stressful situation. In addition to the weight of his legal responsibilities, the uneasiness that was associated with military duty, particularly in a conflict zone, was only exacerbated by the situation. During the time that he was getting ready to step down from his position as a judge, he was concerned about the cases that he would be leaving behind as well as the effect that his absence would have on his community.

Struggles and Pressure Faced by Individuals

In addition to the difficulties he encountered in his personal life, McIntyre was also confronted with the realities of military deployment, which added to the emotional burden he was carrying. According to the reports, he was the subject of a federal investigation in connection with a controversy that involved the acquisition of furniture through a military contract. Despite the fact that the specifics of the inquiry are yet unknown, he was under a great deal of strain because of the possibility of facing legal consequences.

Under the scrutiny of the investigation and the coming

deployment, McIntyre's professional life, which had previously been characterised by success and earning the respect of the community, started to disintegrate. This environment of isolation was established as a result of the convergence of various stresses, which included the strain of a military responsibility, the weight of judicial obligations, and the looming prospect of scandal. McIntyre had a difficult time coping with the magnitude of his situation, despite the fact that he was a famous figure and was immersed in the company of his friends and coworkers.

A Tragic Concluding Statement

In a tragic turn of events, Richard Dean McIntyre's life was taken from him on October 30, 2007. His body was discovered at his residence, and it appeared that he had committed himself. He had apparently given in to the immense pressures that had accumulated over the course of the years preceding up to that tragic day. He had only 51 years under his belt.

Those who had known him as

a devoted judge, a military commander, and a family man were particularly affected by the news of his passing, which sent shockwaves through the town of Indiana. The passing of this individual was a tragic event, not only for his family but also for a community that had relied on his leadership and commitment to the pursuit of justice. McIntyre's contributions to the legal system and his unshakeable devotion to serving others were pondered upon by colleagues, friends, and members of the community in the days that followed his passing. These individuals paid respect to McIntyre by expressing their thoughts and feelings.

The Effects That His Funeral Will Have

The suicide of McIntyre sparked significant conversations on mental health, particularly among public servants who frequently struggle under the weight of enormous responsibilities. The stigma that surrounds mental health concerns was brought to light by his passing, particularly within the military and judicial circles, where vulnerability can be seen as a sign of weakness.

Following the news of his passing, many people started looking into the difficulties that judges and military personnel find themselves under. There was an increased emphasis placed on the provision of support systems for those who were employed in high-stress professions. The objective was to establish an atmosphere in which individuals could seek assistance without the fear of being judged or facing professional penalties. The life and death of McIntyre served as a catalyst for change, which in turn prompted conversations about the significance of mental health resources for individuals who are employed in official capacities.

Inheritance of Service as a Legacy

Richard Dean McIntyre left behind a legacy that is characterised by service, integrity, and dedication, despite the unfortunate circumstances surrounding his death. His legacy will live on in his community forever thanks to the achievements he made as a judge and as a military commander. He is remembered for his compassionate approach to the law, as well as his dedication to justice and his efforts to improve the legal process. McIntyre's efforts to reform the judicial process receive widespread recognition.

Additionally, McIntyre's legacy includes the roles that he played as a spouse and a father. He is survived by his wife, Meredith Mettlen, and their three children, who continue to uphold his principles and carry on his legacy. As a way of paying tribute to his life, his family and the community continue to stress the significance of compassion, leadership, and service.

CONCLUSION

The life and career of Richard Dean McIntyre show a complicated tapestry that is weaved from commitment, ambition, and a sad conclusion that has a profound impact not only inside his community but far beyond it. We are reminded of the complex nature of public service and the often-hidden challenges that accompany it as we reflect on McIntyre's journey, which began with his early hopes to serve as a Navy pilot and culminated in his important career as a lawyer, politician, and judge.

A Legacy Comprised of Many Facets

His commitment to the values of justice, duty, and community service is what defines McIntyre's legacy. His political objectives and judicial decisions are not the only things that characterise his legacy; rather, it embraces all of these things. Through the entirety of his political career, he shown an unflinching dedication to the people he represented in Indiana, and he navigated the turbulent waters of politics with drive and resilience. It was during his time as a judge that he made decisions that would have a significant impact on the lives of a great number of people, which further demonstrated his dedication to fairness and integrity.

When it comes to the sphere of public service, the narrative of McIntyre is representative of the sacrifices that many people who serve in elected and appointed posts make without hesitation. The weight of responsibility, the scrutiny of public life, and the unrelenting demands of leadership can all contribute to the creation of considerable pressures that, in some instances, can become overpowering. The issues that people in high-stress occupations confront in terms of their mental health are brought to light by his life, which serves as a powerful reminder of the importance of such understanding.

The significance of support systems

Because of the unfortunate circumstances surrounding McIntyre's passing, important discussions concerning mental health have been spurred, notably within the military and the legal communities. As a result, it highlights the importance of having solid support systems that put an emphasis on mental well-being and give individuals with the resources they require to successfully traverse the obstacles that come with their roles. It is essential, in order to prevent tragedies of a similar nature, to establish a setting in which public servants are able to freely communicate their troubles, seek assistance without fear of being stigmatised, and have access to mental health resources.

As we pay tribute to McIntyre's legacy, it is of the utmost importance that we push for programs that raise awareness about mental health, inspire resilience, and promote open discourse about the challenges that are encountered by those who serve the public. By doing so, we are not only paying homage to the legacy that McIntyre has left behind, but we are also working towards the goal of preventing others from experiencing the same fate.

In the Name of Carrying

On His Legacy

Richard Dean McIntyre left behind a legacy that will continue to be carried on by the principles he advocated for and the influence he exerted during his life. Everyone who knew him, including his family, friends, and coworkers, will always remember him as a man of principle, a public servant who was dedicated to his work, and a loving husband and father. The principles that he inculcated in his offspring and the understandings that he gained from his own life will serve as a beacon of light for subsequent generations.

While it is important to acknowledge the accomplishments that McIntyre made, it is as important to keep in mind that his life was more than the circumstances surrounding his passing. His journey is illustrative of the commitment, sacrifice, and difficulties that many people struggle with in order to achieve their goals of making a difference in their communities. We pay tribute to his memory and contribute to a more empathetic understanding of the complexity of public service by participating in activities that celebrate his accomplishments and advocate for changes to existing systems.

Made in United States
Troutdale, OR
11/29/2024

25441231R00046